PICTURE PERFECT DOGS

A GUIDE TO DOG PHOTOGRAPHY

STEVE ELTINGE

MIP PUBLISHING

MONTECITO, CALIFORNIA

Many Thanks to Vincent Quaranta

Library of Congress Cataloging in Publication Data
-Eltinge, Steve.
Picture Perfect Dogs: A Guide to Dog Photography
Published by MIP Publishing, P. O. Box 50632, Montecito, California 93150
Manufactured in the United States of America

ISBN: 0-9617204-2-5

Photography:

STEVE ELTINGE

Technical Editing:

PAULA BAKER
STEVE BOYAJIAN
PAUL BREAKSTONE
JAMES HECK

Copy Editing:
SASHA NEWBORN
ELIZABETH VOGT

(Kodachrome 64)

TABLE OF CONTENTS

(Kodachrome 200)

INTRODUCTION

Almost everyone knows what a good picture looks like. Have you ever noticed how quickly people apologize when they hand you a stack of snapshots? "I'm sorry about these but . . . I took them in a hurry . . . It was an ugly day . . . My daughter dropped the camera . . . My husband took them." Here's my favorite: "I'm sorry about these, they were taken with a cheap camera." We act as though there were an unwritten standard of excellence for photography to live up to. Of course, there is no such standard, but there are some simple procedures anyone can learn to help produce excuse-free images. And that is what this book is all about.

Not only will you learn to take pictures to be proud of, you'll also learn techniques to deal with one of the most challenging of photographic subjects — the dog. Any professional photographer will tell you that taking pictures of children and animals requires a great deal of patience. Dogs in particular exhibit a wide range of behavior and emotion. While the reclining cat or the perched bird regard a probing camera with indifference, the dog is ever aware of its surroundings and often reacts in unpredictable ways. Don't let this discourage you, because some basic rules of photography, along with a few simple strategies for controlling a dog's behavior, will allow you to take memorable photographs of your pet. Once these simple skills become habit you will be forever free from the anxiety of *hoping* that "the film turns out."

Read Chapter One first, *WHAT'S WRONG WITH THIS PICTURE?*. If you can become a critical observer of the objects in the viewfinder *before* you release the shutter, you have mastered half of the task of taking a good picture.

Making a decision about which camera to buy, what film to select, and how and when to use strobe light is covered in Chapter Two, *THE RIGHT TOOLS*. Know your alternatives before you go to the camera store.

Chapters Three and Four offer some advanced ideas for those who wish to take pictures for advertising, for exhibition or simply for the joy of creating images that please the eye.

This book does not cover specialized topics such as diffusing light, fill cards, or repetitive strobe effects. If you are ready for advanced photographic techniques, then you have already reached a level of accomplishment beyond the scope of this book. The subject of filtration, particularly special effect filtration, belongs to "gimmick photography," and probably has little value for the picture-taking you will do of dogs.

Throughout the pages that follow, there are numerous photographs of pure-bred dogs; however, I must admit that my personal bias about breeds is apparent. As a Staffordshire Bull Terrier owner, and a photographer who loves the "Bull Breeds," it was difficult for me not to dip into a stockpile of "Bully" photographs and share a few extra with you. In particular, the French Bulldog puppy on the cover was a delight to work with, and he deserves a special pat for helping me produce one of my favorite photographs.

I've spent most of my adult life photographing dogs, and my experiences have been filled with equal amounts of laughter and frustration; I know that I must always expect the unexpected. The only certainty in working with a dog is that your subject will never be anything other than what you see. That kind of honesty has to be appealing to anyone who holds a camera.

(Plus-X)

From the desk of Linda...

Dear Valerie,
    Finally our new puppy is here. I
don't know who's more excited — the
kids or Bob!
    We've _____ to name her Rosey
after my _____
enjoy her _____
    Anyw_____
we pro_____
both a_____
can't _____
next _____
Bob a_____
with the puppy
all afternoon playing with _____
only two good shots.

                              Love, Linda

CHAPTER ONE

WHAT'S WRONG WITH THIS PICTURE?

Dear Linda:

We got your picture. — Thank you.
It's hard to believe how Jeremy has grown. And little Allison, my gosh, she's taller than a trash can. Did you put a new roof on the house since our last visit? From your comments it sounds like you're excited about the new dog. Could you send us another photo — maybe one that shows a little more detail? — The head and body would do nicely.

Just as computers never make mistakes, cameras never take bad pictures. A camera is simply a tool, but put the same tool in different hands, and you will see totally different results. In a sense, you must show your camera what to see. The skills needed to take a good photograph are few, and they are surprisingly easy to master. Keep in mind that a roll of twenty-four exposures is expensive, and it costs just as much to process a bad photograph as it does a good one. Besides, how many times has someone handed you stacks of snapshots with the expectation that you will leaf through them with enjoyment and enthusiastic commentary, while your private thoughts beg for the courtesy of being handed two or three quality photographs worth looking at? You can go a long way toward assuring yourself that your viewers won't be subjected to this kind of monotony by learning some guidelines to help evaluate your photography.

Throw It Away

Too many people have a mental block about disposing of bad photographs. No matter how good the image could have been, if it is grossly under-or-overexposed, throw it away. No matter how appealing the subject matter, if it is out of focus, throw it away. If you have taken five shots of the same thing and one is clearly better than the others, why ask your viewer to look at all five? Throw four away. You can practice the "Throw It Away" exercise by going back through some of your old snapshots. Don't get sentimental. If they are bad, throw them away. Keeping images for posterity is self-trickery. The next generation to view your bad photographs will undoubtedly share the majority of them with the trash can.

Clutter

Eliminating clutter is the first step toward creating simplicity in a photograph; let the viewer see only what is important. Linda's photograph on the opening page of this chapter is filled with clutter, and it would have taken just a moment's forethought to correct this problem. Occasionally, you have no control over the unwanted objects in front, behind or around your subject. But most of the time, distractions can be minimized by placing the subject in front of a simple background. Clean landscaped yards, isolated beaches, open fields, parks, or other natural areas free from litter are all good settings. When cluttered surroundings are unavoidable, stand the dog above your eye level, so that you can use the sky as natural background.

Another way to eliminate clutter is to move in close to the subject; a *tight shot* minimizes the number of unwanted objects in the background.

Clean landscaped yards, isolated beaches, open fields, parks, or other natural areas free from litter are all good settings. (Plus-X)

If you cannot eliminate unwanted clutter, use the sky as a background. (Plus-X)

Finally, there is a more advanced technique for eliminating clutter from your photography—manipulating the *depth of field*. This technique is discussed in detail in Chapter Three. Most of the time, however, controlling depth of field is less helpful than locating a simple background for your dog.

Another approach is the creative use of clutter. Sometimes extraneous background objects can add impact to your photograph. Take, for instance, the picture on the opposite page of a Doberman Pinscher in an automobile wrecking yard. Normally, you wouldn't consider this appealing. But in this photo, the chaotic assemblage of metal parts and tires is a striking contrast to the elegance and symmetry of this handsome animal.

The chaotic assemblage of metal parts and tires is a striking   (Tri-X)
contrast to the elegance and symmetry of this handsome animal.

The Tight Shot

A photo taken when close to the subject is called *shooting tight* or creating a *tight shot*. Notice how television camera operators maintain a *tight shot*. They fill the viewing area with the subject and nothing else. So don't be afraid to move in. You will discover very interesting images from a perspective that you might think is uncomfortably close. This is especially true with animal photography. A shot of the eyes can be captivating, and a very tight shot will often produce wonderful results.

A   (Plus-X)   *B*   (Plus-X)

Even when backgrounds are appealing, they can spoil a good photograph by taking up too much of the image area. Photograph A (above left) is free from clutter and there is nothing unpleasant about the background; but notice in photograph B how much more impact is achieved by moving in close. In a sense, you actually size or *crop* the image even before you develop the film.

Even though the dog is the main subject in this photograph, (Kodachrome 25)
*a **tight shot** would be much less interesting.*

17

*A **very** tight shot will often produce wonderful results.* (Fujichrome 50)

Focus

The practice of focusing correctly seems so fundamental that it should not need separate discussion, yet I am continually amazed to see how often people will purchase expensive advertising space in national dog magazines and then submit a blurred image. Out-of-focus pictures result from one of three preventable problems: inaccurate focusing by the camera operator, camera movement, or subject movement.

18

What's Wrong with This Picture?

Camera operators who consistently have difficulty focusing can improve their work by purchasing an automatic focus, 35mm camera. Autofocus cameras have become very popular, and are a special blessing for photographers who wear glasses. Some automatic focus cameras produce excellent results in situations where the subject moves faster than you can maintain focus.

If you focus manually, look through the viewfinder of your camera, and you will see either a *split image* system or a *central grid* system. The *split image* system requires that you focus on a precise visual point of reference. For example, fix your eye on a vertical part of the dog, such as an ear or front leg. Notice that this point of reference appears to be broken in half. Adjust the focusing ring until this broken or *split image* is whole. In the case of close-up photography, you must focus on a smaller object: hair, eyelashes, or pupils of the eye work well.

The more common type of manual focusing system is called the *central grid* (or central microprism). When you look through the viewfinder at an unfocused subject, you will notice that the entire viewing area appears blurred. Unlike the split image focusing system, the center of the focusing grid consists of many microprisms which blur the subject if they are not aligned correctly. Turn the focusing ring slowly, and you will notice these small prisms converge into sharp focus. Allow your eye to focus beyond, in front of, and then directly on the subject. In this way, you can be certain that your final point of focus is exact.

Camera motion is the most frequent cause of a blurred or soft image, and it happens regardless of the type of camera you own. Using a tripod or monopod is the best way to steady a camera, but in many situations tripods and monopods are not practical. In such cases, you need to learn to brace your hand-held camera by leaning against a solid support such as a tree, a car, or a wall, or standing or sitting in one of the following postures:

Bracing your camera is especially important in low-light situations because the lens will be open for a long time. This is true for both automatic and manually operated cameras.

Finally, a subject which moves faster than your camera's shutter will be blurred on the negative. Unless your dog is very old, meditating, sleeping or in the field pointing, it is probably in motion most of the time. Even dogs that have been set in a posed stance cannot refrain from moving their tails, blinking their eyes, fidgeting, or exposing (forgive the pun) their tongues. A dog's tongue is especially annoying because it darts out with such rapidity that the photographer usually discovers this doggie gesticulation *after* the film has been processed! The lesson here is to take more photographs than you think you need. This message will be repeated often in this book and with good reason. Bowls of fruit and pretty flowers are a sure thing. But with dogs, what you see is very often not what you get. If you think you got the shot the first time, take a few more.

A subject related to focusing is the quality of the prints made from your negatives. There are limitations to the size and quality of the final image produced from a 35mm negative, regardless of how well you focused the camera. Professional photographers are always aware of the need to produce crisp images that show abundant detail across the entire subject area and even in the shadows. Of the several variables that contribute to image *sharpness*, the lens is the most important. If you have purchased a camera that does everything automatically, and you paid less than $150, do not expect to take pictures of the same quality as you would if you owned a more expensive 35mm camera.

The film you use will also have an effect upon the quality of the final print. This is especially true if you intend to make prints larger than 5 x 7 inches. With few exceptions, always use a slow film if your intentions are to make large prints. Color print film with an ISO rating of 100 and black & white film with an ISO rating of 100 or 125 are the best films in most circumstances. 100 ISO color film offers rich color saturation, excellent contrast and a likelihood that large prints will remain sharp. 125 ISO black & white film offers the benefit of a broad range of gray tones as well as a sharp image. Very slow film like Ektar 25 can be used when large prints are the objective, but beware of high contrast.

Camera Angles

When it comes to seeing eye-to-eye with a canine subject, Great Danes and Irish Wolfhounds are about the only dogs that qualify. Canines of lesser height are too often photographed from a steep angle that is unflattering and unrealistic. These aerial shots result in images that have an authoritarian bent, preventing the viewer from any emotional attachment to the subject. Further, the photograph of a dog looking up at a hovering lens often appears distorted, its head being too large for the body. This occurs because most of us are used to taking pictures of human beings whose height approximates our own. Correcting poor camera angles takes only a second and you will see simple and dramatic improvement in your pictures.

If the dog is between the size of a Cocker Spaniel and a German Shepherd, it is helpful to get down on one knee. For dogs the size of a Maltese or Dachshund, you must get down on one knee, or even better, lie flat on the ground. An alternative would be to seat the dog on an elevated object.

The Importance of Expression

Purebred dogs recognized by the American Kennel Club and other organizations have descriptive *standards* which detail the physical appearance of each breed; and in virtually every breed there is some discussion of the dog's eyes,

No physical feature affects the expression of a dog more than the eyes. (Ektachrome 100)

often in great detail. No physical feature affects the expression of a dog more than the eyes. When we meet a dog it is important that we make eye contact, if only for a brief moment. Even Old English Sheepdogs or Bouvier des Flandres have eyes hidden behind all the fur and they do make visual contact with you. The eyes communicate a great deal about a dog's character, its health, and even its intentions. For this reason it is a good idea to have the dog facing in the direction of the camera and a better idea to have the dog looking directly down the lens.

When you review your checklist of things to remember before snapping the shutter, make a quick mental assessment of the final image you are about to record. Even if every other element of the photograph is technically sound but the subject is boring, why take the photograph? Determining the precise moment to take a picture, that moment when everything seems to come together, takes a good eye as well as practice.

Red Eye/Green Eye

Red Eye is a term used to describe the ghostly-looking, glowing red eyes of humans (and sometimes dogs) on prints reproduced from film exposed by electronic flash. *Red Eye* results when light passes through the lens of the eye, illuminating the blood vessels on the surface of the retina. This happens most often when the flash unit is close to the camera lens, so that the light reflected off the retina is targeted directly back into the lens of the camera. *Green Eye* is more often seen in the eyes of dogs and cats. When light passes through the iris of a dog's eye, it strikes a cellular layer of tissue called the Tapetum, and then reflects back onto the film. The Tapetum acts as a kind of mirror which usually projects fluorescent green light, and is most visible in night photography. If you own a camera with a dedicated flash (one which is built into the body of the camera) there are a couple of things you can do to solve the problem of red eye/green eye: one is to turn the camera slightly away from the subject, so that light reflected by the flash does not converge on the center of the lens of the eye; a second trick is to apply transparent adhesive tape over the face of the flash unit, thus diffusing (softening) the light that hits the subject. If you attach your flash unit to the camera via a bracket (hot shoe) or synch cord, simply remove the flash from the camera body and hold it a foot or two away from the lens; or bounce the light from the flash off a wall or ceiling.

To avoid red eye/green eye simply remove the flash from the camera body and hold it a foot or two away from the lens.

Conquering Shadows

I have often thought Rembrandt would have been an excellent photographer, because fine art photography is, after all, simply painting with light. In this sense light can become a photographer's greatest ally. For the skilled photographer, light is more than mere illumination; it is a tool that can add intensity and emotion to an otherwise boring photograph. Light enhances or subdues color, softens shadows, emphasizes detail.

In this photograph, the woman's shadow falls across the Poodle,   (Plus-X)
seriously detracting from the intended outcome.

By repositioning the two subjects, the dog becomes a point of interest, and its dark coat shows greater detail.

(Plus-X)

Light literally points the way to what is important in a photograph and leaves to shadows the job of framing the message in tones that range from soft gray to black.

Noticing shadows is not always easy. Be especially cautious about placing a dog to the shadow side of its handler. When photographing two dogs, the one on the sun side will often cast a shadow on the other. This problem becomes more apparent when the dog on the sun side is light, and the darker dog stands in its shadow. Blocking shadows also occur when one dog is much larger than another.

The Horizon Line

If you're one of those people who compulsively straightens crooked paintings hung on walls, you needn't read this section. For you, the practice of leveling the horizon in the viewfinder will come naturally. For the rest of us, however, aligning the subject perpendicular to the horizon is a good habit to learn, since it is not only fundamental to good photography, but is the way most of us see the world.

If you are outdoors, the horizon itself should be the point of reference for correctly holding the camera. If you cannot identify the horizon or you are indoors, search for perpendicular objects against which to align your camera. Building corners, door frames, tree trunks and sidewalks are generally reliable. Even a dog can be used, since dogs are most comfortable sitting or standing perpendicular to the ground or floor.

If you have taken an excellent picture and the horizon is sloping, all is not lost since faulty horizon lines are one of the easier things to remedy when prints are made from negatives. Prevention, however, is always best.

Summing it up

Here's is a brief checklist of things to ask yourself before exposing all that expensive film:

1. Are all of the technical parts of my camera (film, exposure settings, etc.) ready, so that I don't have to think about them while taking pictures?

2. Is the subject of my photograph properly lit, or are there unwanted shadows?

3. Is there clutter in the background?

4. Am I close enough to the subject to crop out visual information which isn't important to the viewer?

5. Is the subject in focus?

6. Am I shooting at a speed fast enough so that I don't have to worry about camera or subject movement?

7. Have I placed the camera at a good angle in relation to the subject?

8. Is my strobe-light positioned to prevent red eye?

9. Have I set the shutter speed on my camera to correctly synch with the flash unit?

10. Is the horizon line correct?

This action-packed image was selected from several in a series. (Kodachrome 25)
It was taken with a 35mm camera connected to a motor drive

CHAPTER TWO

THE RIGHT TOOLS

There are only three tools necessary to take a photograph: a camera, film and light. The list of photographic accessories or supplemental tools is almost unlimited. Meters, light stands, tripods, filters, cases, flash units, etc., all add to the photographer's ability to produce quality images. However, the key is to have the right tools to produce the best results while maintaining portability, efficiency, and simplicity.

With dog photography, time is not your ally. Each second wasted in an attempt to manipulate complex equipment might be the second your subject gets away or loses interest. If you are shopping for *the right tools* for dog photography, simplicity must be at the top of your list of requirements.

The Camera

More than anything else, people want to know which camera to buy. There are dozens of cameras to choose from, and the technology is changing so rapidly that by the time this book goes into print there will undoubtedly be some innovative developments not discussed here. Twenty years ago it was easy to

Small (35mm)   *Medium Format*   *View Camera* (Plus-X)
Camera   *Camera*

answer the question, who makes the best camera? Names like Nikon and Leica were the world standards. This is no longer true. Today, Canon, Ricoh, Minolta, Olympus, Pentax and others can be added to the list of excellent cameras.

Before going into detail about 35mm cameras, let me at least mention several other camera options with larger film sizes. These are called medium and large format. Next to 35mm, medium format is the most popular choice among professional and accomplished amateur photographers. Medium format cameras have the advantage of offering a big negative (6 x 4.5 centimeters, 6 x 6 cm or 6 x 7 cm). These negatives produce large prints with exceptional clarity and rich color.

Medium format cameras are expensive, however. They are also complicated to use and weigh a great deal more than 35mm cameras.

Large format is also available, but rarely used for spontaneous animal photography. The most common (and smallest) negative size for large format is 4 x 5 inches. Other large format negatives are 5 x 7, 8 x 10, 11 x 14 and 16 x 20 inches. These extra large film formats are used almost exclusively for technical, architectural, and commercial photography.

At the other end of the film spectrum, there are the miniature sizes — films smaller than 35mm. Most of these films were created for use with small copy and spy cameras and have little application for recreational photography. In fact, 110mm and disc films are about the only subminiature films that can be purchased in most stores. If you are serious about quality photography, 110mm and disc films are not worth considering.

A 35mm camera is the best tool you can buy for most dog photography, regardless of how much money you have to spend or your level of skill. 35mm cameras are light and easy to use which makes them perfect for spontaneous shooting. Most recently, computers have been enlisted to optically design 35mm camera lenses, and many are sharp enough to satisfy even the most critical eye. Lenses for 35mm cameras are also less expensive to purchase than lenses for medium or large format cameras. If a good lens is used, there is no reason why a 35mm negative cannot produce 8 x 10 inch prints that rival medium format for sharpness and detail. In addition, medium format film requires processing in custom photo labs while 35mm film often takes only an hour.

Many 35mm cameras have special capabilities which are unavailable in other formats. Specifically, most 35mm cameras can shoot at speeds of 1/1000 of a second or faster, which is ideal for action photography. Some of the new and

4 x 5

6 x 7

2 ¹⁄₄

35mm

These excellent cameras (as well as others not pictured here) are priced under $300, and have more than enough capability to produce quality images.

more expensive 35mm cameras shoot at speeds up to 1/8000 which means that, theoretically, the titanium shutter is capable of opening and closing 8000 times in less than a second. Even a speeding bullet would have trouble evading the rapid precision of a shutter moving this fast.

The variety of film available for 35mm cameras is also broader than that offered for larger format cameras, and the number of frames per role in 35mm film is greater. The availability of film is another consideration; almost every grocery or convenience store carries 35mm film in 12, 24 and 36 exposures.

So, 35mm is the right format. But which 35mm camera? There are manual mode cameras, programmable cameras, automatic cameras, and cameras which allow the photographer to choose between programmable, automatic and manual modes. Frankly, some of the modern programmable cameras have become so sophisticated that they are more difficult to understand than a manually operated camera. The irony here is that they were designed to make life easy for the amateur photographer. If you want true simplicity, there are cameras that load the film, interpret film speed automatically, read the available light, focus, know when to trigger the automatic flash, and rewind the film at the end of the roll. If you want a quality camera that does the thinking for you, you should expect to pay between $200 and $350. You can buy cameras which have these features for less money, but beware of poor lens quality, lack of reliability, questionable durability, and creative limitations.

If you are a bit more enthusiastic about the technical aspects of cameras, you might want to think about purchasing a camera that will accept a wide variety of accessories, such as lenses, winders and motor drives. Most cameras of this caliber have both an automatic and manual mode, and many can be purchased secondhand for reasonable prices.

This is a good time to introduce some basic information about the technical side of cameras. Like every other specialization, photography has a technical vocabulary to describe just about every aspect of picture taking. It is this vocabulary or "special language" that stops many creative people from wanting to learn more about their camera. This is unfortunate, because the extent of the "special language" that one needs to know is very limited and should not deter enthusiastic beginners from enjoying the creative experience of a camera with manual settings.

1. *Lens length* is the first descriptive term a camera and lens buyer may encounter. The annoying part about this description is that it has nothing to do with how long the lens is. Actually *lens length* is more accurately described as *focal length*. Short lenses or lenses with a *short focal length* bring into focus a wider or broader angle of view. *Very short focal length* lenses are called *wide-angle* lenses. Long focal length lenses are called telephoto lenses, and those in between are medium focal length lenses.

    Wide-angle lenses range from 20mm or less (a fisheye lens) up to about 35 millimeters. Medium-length lenses range from about 40mm to 135mm. Long lenses go from 135mm to over 1000mm. If you are in the camera store and you hear a customer say, "I'd like to look at some of your medium focal length lenses," you will know that he or she wants to look at lenses that are between 40mm and 135mm.

2. *Aperture* and *F-stop* are the two words that newcomers to the field of photography seem to dislike more than any others. An *aperture* is a hole centered in the lens through which light passes on its way to exposing the film. The size of the aperture or hole is determined by the photographer, or by the camera if it is a "fully automatic camera." The

aperture is adjusted to be larger or smaller depending upon the amount of light that is being reflected from the subject to the camera lens. Think about the way the pupils of your eyes react to light. If there is a lot of light, your pupils get small. In a dark room your pupils expand. The aperture in your camera mimics this process.

Someone somewhere decided that we needed to have a name to describe the different size apertures. This name is F-stop. Technically, an F-number or F-stop refers to a mathematical ratio between the lens diameter and its focal distance. All you need to know is that the F-stops on a Minolta lens are the same as they are on a Ricoh lens or on a Nikon lens, and so forth. F-stops have been assigned numerical values which range from f/1.0 to f/64 and there are twelve or so increments in between. Here's the really frustrating part: the bigger the F-stop number, the smaller the hole (*aperture*) and vice versa. For example f/2.8 is a very large aperture, while f/22 is very small. An F-stop of 8 is about in the middle on most *medium length* 35mm lenses. If someone suggests that you "open up" the lens, they mean for you to make the aperture bigger by moving the F-stop ring to a smaller number like f/4. If they suggest that you "stop down" the lens, you will want to search for a big F-stop number like f/16 or f/22. By the way, you really aren't "opening up" or "stopping down" the lens, you are manipulating a movable diaphragm built inside the lens.

3. *Shutter speed* is one of the simpler concepts with which you need to become familiar, and you can take satisfaction in knowing that this is a very straightforward expression. Shutter speed simply means the speed at which the shutter in your camera opens and closes. On most 35mm cameras, the shutter speed indicator is located on top of the camera. If you set the shutter of your camera at 125, you can expect that it will

A (Plus-X)

B (Plus-X)

(Plus-X)

Photograph A was shot at f/16. Notice that this small aperture brings all 3 dogs into focus. In photograph B, the camera was focused on the middle dog and shot at f/4 causing the front and back dogs to fall out of focus. In photograph C, the front dog was shot at f/2.8 which resulted in the other dogs becoming a blur.

open and shut very quickly, allowing just a small amount of light to be reflected on the film. If you set your camera at 1, the shutter will open and stay open for a full second before it closes again. A full second allows a lot of light to hit the film, something you almost never want to do in dog photography. In fact, most of the shutter settings you use will be at 60 and above. You may want to know what the shutter speed numbers like 1, 60, 125, mean. They are a fractional measure of a second. 1 is one second, 60 is a 60th of a second, and 125 is 125th of a second.

4. *Depth of Field* is the last of the essential things to know. *Depth of field* refers to the area or zone which is in sharp focus. Even though it may appear to your eye that everything in the viewfinder is in focus, the lens on your camera may not "see it" that way. If the aperture has been set for f/4 (a large lens opening), the *depth of field* will be very shallow. In other words, the zone of focus will be limited. The interplay between film speed, aperture and shutter speed helps determine the *depth of field.* The three photographs on pages 40 and 41 visually illustrate how depth of field can be used to eliminate backgrounds. One of the trade-offs for choosing to de-emphasize the background is that the area of correct focus is diminished, forcing the photographer to be absolutely precise when focusing on the subject. Almost every 35mm camera has a *depth of field* preview button which will let you see what part of your subject is or is not in focus. In addition, every lens has a *depth of field scale* imprinted adjacent to the focusing ring.

If you have a conceptual grasp of the last few paragraphs, then you have overcome a major hurdle in your understanding of how a camera works. Lens (focal) length, aperture, F-stop and shutter speed are all interrelated. If you can learn to manipulate them correctly, you can stop taking snapshots and begin making photographs.

The Lens

It is highly recommended that lens quality be the top priority with any camera you purchase. This is as true for fully automatic cameras as it is for those which are manually operated. If you own only one lens it should be a zoom lens which covers a focal length of 35mm to 90mm. You will rarely need a wide angle lens (any lens less than 40mm) for dog photography. The exception might be a shot where the dog is in the foreground and the background is of such panoramic beauty that it must be included as well. If you are purchasing lenses with fixed focal lengths, such as 50mm, 135mm, etc., you will want to own at least three: 50mm, 85 or 90mm, and a long lens (180mm to 250mm). The 50mm lens is a normal focal length: it reproduces approximately what is seen with the human eye. The 85mm to 105mm lens is a portrait lens and the one you will probably use most often. This lens will allow you to stand at a comfortable distance from a dog (about the same distance you would stand when using a 50mm lens) and yet frame the subject tight in the viewfinder. A telephoto lens is a long lens and is also ideal for dog photography. Long lenses make it possible to take candid shots from a distance.

A few words are in order here about zoom lenses. Zoom lenses are specially constructed to allow the camera operator to change the focal length and angle of view. The advantage of this lens is that the camera operator does not have to change position in order to take in a broader or narrower view of the subject area. This is a feature you will use often, especially when the dog is in motion or you need to make a quick decision about whether or not to eliminate the background.

Because of the design of most zoom lenses, more glass must be used in their manufacture. This requires the light to pass through more pieces of glass before it reaches the film plane, thus diminishing the quality of the image. In addition, the more glass, the heavier the lens. Many who are knowledgeable about cameras argue that zoom lenses have greatly improved over the past ten

180mm

85mm

50mm

28mm

years, and for most small format photography it is difficult to detect the difference between images taken by a quality fixed focal length lens and a quality zoom lens. Zoom lenses offer the photographer convenience and flexibility. If you must "travel light," yet need a variation in focal lengths, then a zoom lens is the right choice.

For the ultimate in convenience, you might consider the purchase of one of the new 35mm fully automatic cameras that have a zoom lens built into the camera body. These cameras do just about everything for you; this includes the freedom to zoom "in" or "away" from the subject with instantaneous, automatic focusing. *Follow focus* is another feature you may want to ask about when purchasing your new camera. *Follow focus* will allow you to follow a moving subject and remain in focus until you are ready to release the shutter. Besides their remarkable technical capabilities, many of these cameras are small and surprisingly light weight.

Film

There are two basic categories of film: slide film and negative film. Choosing the correct film to purchase has a lot to do with your intentions for the finished product. For most of us, slide film (transparency or chrome film — Koda*chrome*, Fuji*chrome*, etc.) is not our first choice. The tolerances for correctly exposing slide film are narrow, and the end product, a slide, can only be shared effectively by using a slide projector. If you already have some favorite "doggie" shots on slide film, these can be made into prints directly either through a print process called Type R, or by a more expensive direct print process called Cibachrome. Transparencies (slides) can also be made into prints by requesting your lab or photo store to have an internegative made from your slide, and then a print (this process is called Type C). The sequence of going from slide back to negative and then to print is costly, but usually produces the best results.

If you begin with *negative* film (Agfa*color*, Koda*color*, Fuji*color*, etc.) you will have the basic material from which to make prints directly. Almost every community now has one-hour processing labs which offer fast processing and quality that almost always surpasses Polaroid prints.

Print film (both black & white, and color) comes in a variety of speeds. *Film speed* refers to the amount of time it takes for the sensitive film emulsion to respond to light (film speed should not be confused with shutter speed). Film speeds are rated by an international code called ISO. For example, Ilford FP4 Black & White film (made in England) is rated ISO 125/22. These rating numbers correspond to two numeric codes once used by competing film manufacturers. All you need to know is that ISO 100 is the color print film speed used most often by most photographers for most situations. ISO 25 is slow film and ISO 400 is fast film; and there is a broad range of speeds available for almost every conceivable photographic situation.

So the next question is: "When should I use slow film and when should I use fast film?" Slow film has some important advantages. First, it offers rich, saturated colors and great detail, so that you can order large prints from slow film negatives without fear of losing sharpness. This is true for both color and black & white films. To date, the slowest color print film available is Ektar 25. *A good rule to remember is to shoot the slowest film that you possibly can in any given situation.* In other words, shoot the slowest film that your subject and available light will allow. There are special circumstances where you may want to shoot faster film for artistic effect, to overcome poor or low light conditions, to diminish high-contrast lighting, or freeze action. Otherwise, there is no point in shooting faster than ISO 100 in color or black & white.

The principal disadvantage of slow film has to do with its response or reaction to light. Skies darkened by inclement weather, subjects in full shade, and fast

Fujichrome 50

Fujichrome 100

Fujichrome 1600

The three photographs on this page were taken with different speed films, at nearly the same time of day and under identical, natural lighting conditions. Notice that the difference in color and contrast between the ISO 50 and ISO 100 is minimal. On the other hand, ISO 1600 shows an obvious shift in color, less contrast, and more graininess.

action photography all inhibit the effectiveness of slow film. Slow film also produces negatives and transparencies that have a high degree of contrast. The slower the film, the more likely it is that you will see beautifully illuminated detail in lighted areas and total darkness in shadows. These situations are the exceptions, however, and should not deter you from shooting slow film most of the time.

If "freezing the action" is your primary goal, you must use fast film. For example, if you're going to the Whippet races take film rated at least ISO 400. Its quick response to light will allow you to shoot at very fast shutter speeds. If you are shooting a litter of free-romping, eight-week old puppies, a roll of ISO 400 will help guarantee that you freeze the action and retain excellent depth of field. But there is a trade-off when you opt for fast film. Specifically, colors will not be reproduced with the same realism your eye enjoyed; they may seem a bit "flat," that is, lacking in contrast (fast film also shows less contrast in black & white). In addition, when you make large prints from fast film negatives, the prints will appear grainy. In some cases, this is a desirable artistic effect, but be sure that it was intentional.

The qualities of films produced by different manufacturers varies widely; choosing a suitable film is a matter of preference. Fujicolor (print film) and Fujichrome (slide film) are excellent films that lean toward heavy color saturation. Kodachrome 25 (slide film) is probably the finest film you can buy; especially in terms of excellent color reproduction and shadow detail. It is almost always the standard against which all new films are judged. However, Kodachrome 25 is a very slow film, requiring excellent lighting conditions. Kodak also manufactures Kodachrome 64, which is twice as fast, and Kodachrome 200 for special situations. Very few photographic laboratories process Kodachrome, so don't be in a hurry to get your film. If you are in a hurry, shoot Ektachrome, Agfachrome or Fujichrome; these films can usually be processed in a few hours by

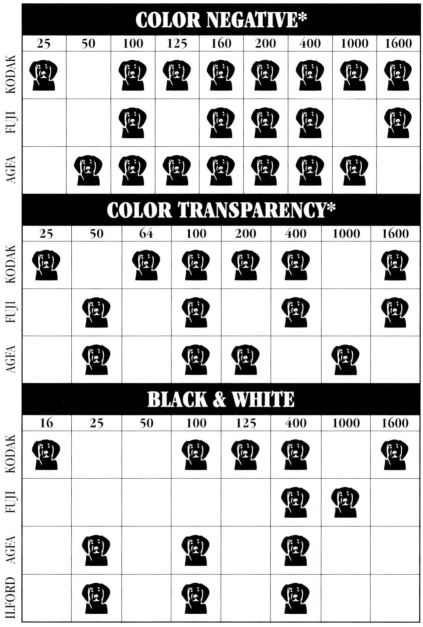

COLOR NEGATIVE*

	25	50	100	125	160	200	400	1000	1600
KODAK	✔		✔	✔	✔	✔	✔	✔	✔
FUJI			✔		✔	✔	✔		✔
AGFA		✔	✔	✔	✔	✔	✔	✔	

COLOR TRANSPARENCY*

	25	50	64	100	200	400	1000	1600
KODAK	✔		✔	✔	✔	✔		✔
FUJI		✔		✔		✔		✔
AGFA		✔		✔	✔		✔	

BLACK & WHITE

	16	25	50	100	125	400	1000	1600
KODAK	✔			✔	✔	✔		✔
FUJI						✔	✔	
AGFA		✔		✔		✔		
ILFORD		✔		✔		✔		

*Daylight Balanced

most custom labs. If you shoot only print film, purchase a 12-exposure roll of Fujicolor and one of Kodacolor. Shoot both rolls of the same subject, under the same lighting conditions, and then have them processed at the same time at a one-hour lab. This small investment will give you an opportunity to evaluate each film according to your preference.

Light

A photographer with a simple box camera who understands how to manipulate light, can take award-winning pictures. One of the best ways to learn how light affects what we see is to spend a few hours in a museum studying the paintings of famous artists. Notice how they use light (or the absence of light) to create a mood. What part of the painting attracts your eye first? Chances are, it has something to do with where and how the artist uses light for emphasis.

It may seem odd to think about it in this way, but the absence of light is the best way to evaluate its presence. In other words, it is important to become a student of shadows. Once you begin to *really* see shadows you will notice that they are not simply black or anti-light. Like light itself, shadows represent a broad range of grays. Master photographers learn to select or create scenes where variations in shadows add tonality and drama to their photographs. The famous nature photographer, Ansel Adams, was such a master.

There are several kinds of light, each of which has a unique effect upon film. Sunlight, moonlight and firelight are natural light, whereas artificial light ema-nates from sources such as light bulbs, fluorescent lights, tungsten-halogen lamps and electronic flash (flash bulbs are a tool of the past). Film manufactur-ers sell film that has been created (*balanced* is the word they use) for either sunlight or artificial light. These two kinds of film are called *daylight* and *tungsten*. Daylight film is created to accurately reproduce colors reflected by sunlight or electronic flash; and tungsten film is created to respond correctly to the kind of light produced by the average household lightbulb.

These Australian Cattle Dogs posed for a photograph that was (Fujichrome 50)
taken with film rated ISO 50 (very slow film), resulting in
saturated color that appears almost unreal.

ISO 50 was also used to capture this active scene with Border (Fujichrome 50)
Collies. Had this photograph not been taken on a day with full sunlight, the film's response time to light would have been insufficient to stop the action. Contrast is another characteristic of slow film, which is illustrated in this picture by the difference between brilliant water highlights and the dogs' dark coats.

This normally white terrier has a yellow cast caused by (Fujichrome 100)
exposing daylight film in a room illuminated by tungsten lamps.

There are very few situations where you will choose to photograph dogs with tungsten lighting. Tungsten lights require long exposures, and if you own dogs you know that anything more than a fraction of a second can be an eternity for tail-wagging subjects. Consequently, all of your photography of dogs will be done in direct sunlight, with electronic flash or with a combination of the two. Therefore, you will need to purchase daylight film only. Manufacturers refer to daylight film as Type S.

Shooting in Sunlight

Sunlight is the most challenging light to shoot in, because the sun dictates the conditions under which you work, and these conditions determine the equipment you need, the film you use, and whether or not supplemental flash is necessary. On an overcast day, the sun still provides abundant illumination; however, the clouds or fog act as a huge diffusing screen, eliminating shadows and often producing flat, lifeless images. On a brilliant sunlit day, shadows help produce the illusion of more than two dimensions as well as add contrast.

Changes in the weather can also produce some interesting effects. Too often photographers leave their cameras at home unless the sun is shining. Foggy, overcast or rainy days can help create a special emotion in photographs. The image below of a working Border Collie, and sheep in full winter coat, was taken on a cold, foggy morning creating a mood that would be absent on a sunny day.

Foggy, overcast or rainy days can help create a special emotion in photographs   (Kodachrome 64)

The quality of light also changes throughout the day. The first hour after sunrise and the last hour before sunset are ideal lighting conditions. The afternoon light in the photograph on the next page adds a warm cast to this otherwise distinctly brindle and white Bull Terrier.

Afternoon light adds a warm cast to this otherwise distinctly brindle and white Bull Terrier.

(Fujichrome 100)

Light and shadow can add dimension even to an all-white subject.

(Kodachrome 64)

The sun can be a source of interest when it is included in the photograph. (Ektachrome 100)

Shooting with Strobe Light

Another source of light that you will use frequently is stroboscopic light, referred to as "strobe light" or "flash" (not to be confused with flash bulbs). This wonderful invention was first introduced to the photographic marketplace in the late 1940s. Since that time electronic flash units have become very portable and easy to understand. In fact, some models are completely automatic. If you own or are considering the purchase of one of the smaller fully automatic cameras, you will be pleased to find that most of them have built-in flash units which provide electronic flash without your assistance. In a manner of speaking, these cameras with built-in flash units "think for themselves"—they know when the natural or ambient light is insufficient, and automatically provide additional light with the flash.

If you own a manually operated or automatic camera which does not have a dedicated flash unit, there are many versatile and sophisticated flash units which can be purchased and attached to your camera with the use of a *synch cord* or a *hot shoe*. These contact points connect the camera to the flash unit. The *synch cord* is a flexible vinyl-covered wire cord, and the *hot shoe* is a small metal plate found on top of the camera. These external flash units are powered by 1.5 or 9 volt batteries, rechargeable batteries or external battery packs; and most offer you the option of manual or automatic operation.

Electronic flash can be used as a sole light source or in combination with other light sources. More often than you might think, a strobe light has great value — even on a brilliant, sunny day. Its ability to illuminate back-lit subjects and eliminate unwanted shadows created by hard sunlight, makes it a valuable tool. With dog photography, strobe light is indispensable. The short duration of an electronic flash will allow you to deal effectively with a subject in motion. In addition, flash units are portable, produce very little heat, can be multi-directional, illuminate a broad range of distance, and have a long life.

There are some disadvantages to relying upon strobe light exclusively. In particular, you will want to be cautious about the intensity of other kinds of light illuminating your subject at the same time as the flash from the strobe unit. Any other light source besides that from the strobe unit is called *ambient light.* The shutter in most 35mm cameras has been synchronized to open and close at a moderate speed, usually a 60th or 125th of a second. Unfortunately, this is slow enough that both strobe flash and sunlight (*ambient light*) will hit the film plane together. This means that if the subject is in motion, the film will record a double exposure. If it is your intention to freeze the action of a subject on a sunlit day, do not use your flash unit. Instead, purchase high speed film and shoot at a fast shutter speed.

Strobe light is an indispensable tool at a dog show. (Kodachrome 25)

Side

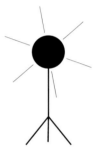

Front

Back

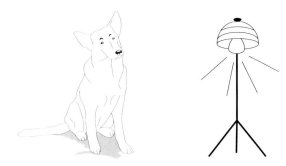

Top

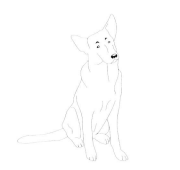

Non-directional

A final word about electronic flash has to do with human error. Film is ruined most often because the camera operator forgot to *synchronize the shutter speed* with the flash unit. Each time the flash is taken out of your camera bag, make flash synchronization the first item to review in your mental check list.

Light Meters

Measuring light is prerequisite to correct exposure. Most of the cameras discussed in this chapter measure light automatically with *through-the-lens metering.* Although convenient in most situations, *through-the-lens light meters* can be tricked by glare or unusual lighting situations such as snow or reflective water surfaces. It is also important to know that light readings are usually

Popular hand held light meters: Strobmeter, Sunlight Meter, Spot Meter.

The brightness of snow can deceive a built-in meter (Kodachrome 25)
*which reads **average** light.*

biased toward the center of the lens. If you point your camera at a dark object centered in a lighter background, chances are the exposure will automatically be set to compensate for the dark object. For example, if you rely on *through-the-lens metering* to dictate the automatic exposure, and you are taking a picture of a dark dog against a lighter background, the dog will be correctly exposed, but the background will be overexposed.

With a little experience, you will be able to estimate with considerable accuracy most outdoor lighting situations without using a light meter if you are using negative film. Slide film, however, *requires* the use of a light meter at all times. Incorrect exposures of more than one half an F-stop with chromatic film will be obvious to anyone viewing the final image. In some cases a professional lab can make exposure corrections on poorly exposed slides, but the amount of correction is limited compared to negative film. Negative film can be processed with reasonable satisfaction even though it is two stops above or below the correct exposure.

If you choose to measure light manually or verify the reading your camera is giving you, you can use an inexpensive handheld light meter. Some of the new meters offer liquid-crystal digital displays and are capable of reading reflected light, incidental light and strobe light. If you are determined to measure light with pinpoint precision (and your subject will stand still in the process) you might want to consider a spot meter. Most spot meters look like small hand guns, and many are capable of reading a very small "spot" of the light falling on the area in the viewfinder. True to their name, spot meters can be pointed at a spot (often less than one degree) in the image area for an exact reading. Spot meters are useful in dog photography when the camera operator is presented with a range of light and shadows that might trick the light meter built into a camera. For example, the spot meter will give an accurate reading of a white dog against a black background or a dark dog silhouetted against a white background or backlit against the sky.

CHAPTER THREE

MAKING A PICTURE

I t has been said that the difference between an amateur photographer and a professional photographer is that "an amateur takes pictures and a professional *makes* pictures." This distinction doesn't pay much respect to the thousands of accomplished amateur photographers who *make* excellent pictures, but it does raise an important point: the best photography is seldom the result of luck. Any photograph imaginable can be created by following the steps (in simplified form) that a motion picture director takes when making a film. Some spontaneity may be lost in this process, but the end result is guaranteed. Study the outstanding photography presented in magazines like *Architectural Digest*, *Elle* and *Esquire*. The photographers whose work appears in these magazines leave nothing to chance. Even images that appear to "capture the moment," like many of those seen in *National Geographic* usually represent a great deal of behind-the-scenes preparation.

When you take the time to sit your dog in front of a field of sunflowers; roll a bright red ball to a group of puppies; or ask a friend to "bait" your new champion with enticing snacks, you are *making* a picture. You have control over the subject and the outcome. What a difference from simply following your dog around the backyard hoping to take one good photograph!

But making a picture requires more than just planning. All of the technical aspects of your camera and accessories must be considered beforehand, so that *nothing* is on your mind except capturing the image you want. You may not get a second opportunity for a great shot; and what a shame to lose the moment because you forgot to cock the shutter or attach a synch cord to the flash.

The photograph of the French Bulldog in the water bowl on the next page is a good example of a planned image. The dog's decision to cool itself in the bowl may have been spontaneous, but the process of capturing the image on film was not. The water bowl was strategically placed to lure the dog after its long hike in the warm afternoon sun, the light had been metered the previous day at a similar time, and the camera readied and correctly positioned on a tripod prior to dog and owner leaving for the hike. All that remained for the photographer to do was wait for the moment when the dog immersed itself, and then release the shutter. Since this shot was *made*, it was possible for the photographer to devote his attention entirely to the subject, rather than fumbling with the camera while the shot got away.

With dogs, you will often discover that control over the subject is a limited luxury regardless of the time and effort spent in preplanning. The best that you can do is to use good judgment in selecting an environment, have command of your equipment, and take as many shots as time, film and the subject will allow.

Photography for Advertising

A few of you who buy this book will do so with the intention of photographing your dog(s) for display in magazines which advertise purebred dogs. If your desire is to create an image to impress dog show judges or capture the attention of prospective puppy buyers, you will want to be certain that the photograph of your dog represents the ideal type according to the breed standard. Photography can be helpful in this pursuit. If your dog has light eyes, avoid direct light;

It appears that the photographer has captured the spontaneous (Plus-X)
action of a French Bulldog cooling itself in a bowl of water, but this
image is actually the result of careful planning.

An advertising photograph that is well-lit and properly composed, will be remembered.

(Fujichrome 100)

if its topline isn't perfect, settle for a shot at a three-quarter angle; if its feet are splayed or pastures down, stand it in grass; if its legs are too short, don't stand it in grass. Because photography can be a permanent record, you will always want to avoid showing your dog's worst side. You are in control; don't settle for anything but a flattering pose. No dog is perfect, so it makes sense to ensure that its faults are never emphasized and its virtues never hidden.

Since this is advertising photography, strive for an image with impact. The standard "show" photograph (handler and stacked dog, with judge holding ribbons) may get looked at, but will it be remembered among dozens of others that look just like it? Be creative. Let your photography tell a story that goes beyond the simple message of Best of Breed. The photograph you take should tell the story without graphic enhancement. If you already subscribe to a specific breed magazine or an all-breed magazine like *Kennel Review*, take a few minutes to study how frequently an eye catching page layout is used to mask a poor photograph. Also note how a simple, beautifully lit and composed photograph is generally complemented with an equally simple graphics background. When a picture must stand alone, it is even more important to compose the image properly and be especially cautious about backgrounds.

Also, consider the page layout and format of the finished product. As a matter of habit, most photographers shoot in *horizontal* format. Practice turning your 35mm camera 90 degrees, into a *vertical* position. This is an essential format for magazine photography, since most magazines are taller than they are wide. The proportions on a 35mm negative are approximately 1 inch wide and 1 1/2 inches high (2.4 cm x 3.6 cm). This is a ratio of 2 to 3 (photographers and graphic artists use the term *aspect ratio* to describe this 2:3 relationship). All you need to remember are the relative proportions when you think about taking a photograph to fit the format of a magazine. If you plan properly, there should be no need to eliminate (crop) any of the image area in your finished picture.

Most of the photographs used for advertising are taken in black & white be-cause black & white images can be reproduced at a fraction of the cost of color. As a photographer you will always want to request black & white prints with a glossy surface. The magazine which accepts your prints will make a *halftone* negative from them. *Halftone negatives* can also be made from color prints, but the end result is a black & white reproduction. If you intend to have the magazine print your final image in color, use transparency film. Magazines that print color rely upon a process called *color separation* which is the color counterpart of the black & white *halftone*. Color separations are made from transparency film more effectively than from a color print. If you must shoot color negative film for purposes of reproduction, have the final image printed on photographic paper with a glossy surface.

If you are shooting for a friend or are shooting stockfile images to sell to publishers or dog-related periodicals, then you MUST know the breed you are photographing. For example, some breeds should be stacked with angulated rear legs, others foursquare; the feet on some should point straight ahead, on others they should turn out slightly; some should have a level topline, others should be roached. There are certain physical characteristics which are the hallmark for individual breeds—most viewers want to see a side shot of a Saluki, a Doberman or an Irish Setter, and a front view of a Bulldog or a Dandie Dinmont Terrier. The idiosyncrasies of each breed are many and may seem insignificant relative to the entire photograph, but they will not escape the critical eye of those who are seriously involved with the breed. Take the time to review the Breed Standards for the dogs you intend to photograph before you submit your photography for publication. Improper grooming on a coated dog, incorrect coat, nose or eye color, poor ear shape or placement, faulty tail set, and even head or body scars, will probably cause the rejection of an otherwise excellent photograph. Pay attention to details when setting up your shoot. Since no dog is perfect, you must create the illusion of perfection. Chalk a White Bull

Some images look best in vertical format ...

... and others in horizontal format.

(Plus-X)

71

Instead of two collies held on leashes, these dogs were allowed to sit (Plus-X)
in a complementary setting. Illumination between the barn doors is
framed in darkness adding an element of visual interest.

Terrier, clip the yellow stains off the chin of a Bearded Collie, clean the debris from the eyes of a white Poodle, trim back the nails on a Doberman, and so forth.

The Dog as a Subject

Every animal photographer's dream is never to have to take a picture of a dog that isn't beautiful, obedience trained, cooperative, and photogenic. This wish list is seldom fulfilled. But even the most unruly of mutts will be special in some way, and it is your challenge to find this better side. The tight shot of the mixed breed on page 64 accentuates its sparkling eyes and clown-like expression. A serious pose of the same dog with a full view of its body would not have the same effect.

Even among pure breeds, there are particular features worth looking at before you take the picture. Breeds with large lips (flews) like Newfoundlands, Great Pyrenees and Boxers often invert their lips, which remain stuck on a dry tooth. Curl your upper lip under and against your top teeth and you will see what I mean. These mastiff-type breeds also tend to drool, a feature that is most unbecoming in a photograph.

It is worth mentioning again that dogs frequently stick their tongues out of their mouths so quickly that it goes unseen by the human eye, but not by the camera. Did you know that dogs have three eyelids? This is true, one below and two above. Rarely, the lower eyelid will come up but frequently the dog shuts its entire eye. Of course, it does no good to say, "and don't blink." You must be prepared to shoot a quantity of film to insure against the blinking eye and the darting tongue. While we are on the subject of things sticking out, you are cautioned to check one extra feature found on the male dog. More than one photographer has had to laugh off their frustration when they review frame after frame of wonderful photography blemished by the projecting penis of an unabashed male dog.

Every dog has a beautiful side. (Plus-X)

Coated and black dogs need special consideration. This is especially true if you are in a room with poor ventilation and an abundance of light, or if you are outdoors and the sun is your principal light source. Since the dog pants to help cool itself, avoid allowing it to get overheated in the first place. This may be difficult to do with a heavy-coated dog, so plan to get your best shots quickly and early in the day.

Dog Psychology

Some variation in temperament between breeds can be expected. Even within each breed or among hybrid dogs, the variations are as diverse as they are among humans. Traditional notions of "typical" breed behavior can be very misleading. I have photographed Rottweilers with personalities one might expect from a Cocker Spaniel, and Cocker Spaniels more ferocious than an attack-trained Shepherd. But some traits are typical of dogs in general. First, they are honest and free from shame. This does not mean that they are free from embarrassment or feelings of humiliation (something to keep in mind when planning a photograph). Most are, by nature, subservient and prefer to take a secondary role behind their masters or an alpha dog. This is especially true when it is confronted with new or unusual situations. Unfortunately, photography places the dog at the center of attention. Often I hear, "I just don't understand it, she never behaves like this at home," or "She always holds her ears up, this is so strange." And how many times have you seen the emcee on television introduce the "singing dog" which doesn't? Most dogs don't have the psychological make-up which allows them to readily transfer "at-home behavior" to strange locations. The message here is to do one of two things: photograph the dog in its home environment, or allow ample time for the dog to familiarize itself with new surroundings. This includes allowing time for the dog to make scent contact with the equipment, the props and anyone that it has not met.

Make friends with the dog just as you would with a child in a portrait session. Before you take the picture you should be able to approach the dog at will with the expectation that it will not change its behavior. Are you relaxed? Dogs are sensitive to the moods of those around them. A nervous dog will drop its head, pin its ears back or pull its head and neck into its shoulders much like a turtle. This lack of confidence always shows up on film. On the other hand, a happy dog offers an alert, intelligent expression, with eyes sparkling.

Once your subject has relaxed, the next step is to create a situation which plays into the dog's keen sense of hearing, sight or scent. If you are taking pictures of your own dog, you are already familiar with the kinds of stimuli that cause it to become alert and offer an attentive, "tuned-in" expression. Dogs with calm personalities like the Mastiff and the Bloodhound respond well to food. Active breeds like Spaniels, Fox Terriers and Chihuahuas come to full attention over sudden, unexpected movement or even a slight unfamiliar noise.

Often, a dog that is normally very active will turn sullen and totally unresponsive during a photo session. Under these circumstances, you need to be especially creative. The photograph on the next page took two sessions before it was possible to get all three dogs to look directly at the camera at the same time. After several exasperating tries with different attention-getting activities, a live rat was used. A wooden plank was placed directly under the camera lens and the rat was allowed to crawl atop the plank. All three dogs instantly riveted their eyes on the rat and the shot was made.

Noise-making devices can be useful but their effectiveness is short-lived. Once a dog has heard a sound, its response diminishes with each successive try. Also, introducing a strange noise does not guarantee that you will prompt the dog to look in the desired direction. High pitched sounds are an excellent way to encourage a dog to use its ears — puppies respond very well to this technique.

Colored Bull Terrier, American Staffordshire Terrier,   (Fujichrome 100)
Staffordshire Bull Terrier

Blowing through the high end of a harmonica, allowing air to pass through the narrow opening of a balloon, a party horn (the kind that unravels with air pressure), or even whistling will work well for a short time. Unexpected sounds, those that represent an intrusion into a dog's territory, are often the best noise stimulus for dogs. This technique requires three people: a photographer, a dog handler and a third person that the dog is not allowed to see. Position yourself and camera so that you are between the dog with its handler and a door or window. Attempt to work in an area that is free from extraneous noise. The third person (unseen by the dog) should be hidden outside the door, window or behind a bush, and ready to tap, knock or rustle leaves when you give a simple verbal cue. Few dogs will fail to respond to this unexpected diversion.

The most consistently successful method for attracting a dog's attention is motion. While this almost always works, it too offers diminishing returns. You must be prepared to get the shot the first or second time or all your efforts may be wasted. Throwing a ball, a hat or a magazine in the air also allows you some control over the direction the dog will be looking.

If you need the dog to focus on an exact spot, it may be necessary to utilize a blind. In this case you will need a third person in the blind to respond to your cue. Anything large enough to conceal a person (a car, trash cans, a small wall, etc.) will work. Strips of paper taped to a broom handle can be exposed from behind the blind and shook in view of the dog when you give the cue. This is very effective. Another, simpler blind is a tall hedge. Few dogs will fail to notice the motion created by the shaking branches of a hedge. Another simple idea for using motion is to ask a friend to walk a previously unseen dog 30 or 40 yards behind your camera when you give the cue. An important point should be mentioned here: Whoever you select to act as a third person—the attention getter—must listen and *follow your cues exactly.* Many potentially good shots are ruined because the attention-getter provided a stimulus too soon or kept it up too long or ad-libbed with sounds that were untimely. In other words, they used their judgment without responding to your direction. When this happens you have lost control and with dogs, control is the key to success.

Scent, sound and sight are the clues to help you map out an effective strategy when making a picture. Remember, with dogs even the best plans have limited usefulness. Dogs have attention spans that seldom last more than 15 minutes, and puppies even less. Be patient. If you fail, it is often better to wait a day and try again instead of forcing the dog through another artificial routine after a thirty-minute break.

(Kodachrome 64)

The Puppy as a Subject

Puppies are a joy. They are gregarious by nature, always inquisitive and quick to respond to new sights, sounds and smells. Puppies function in two modes: sleep and action. When they are not sleeping they are never voluntarily at rest; which means that if you need a puppy to remain still while you set up your camera, you must be prepared to offer it a new toy, a bit of food or anything else which stimulates its curiosity. But move quickly—in a matter of seconds it will lose interest in your stuffed toy, and go bounding off in the opposite direction in pursuit of its own shadow.

All puppies are cute, but those under three weeks of age rarely exhibit enough personality to make them worth a photo session. From three to five weeks (the weaning period) they will begin to feel comfortable about walking away from each other and their mother. This is an ideal time to take pictures because they don't wander far and their movements are usually preceded by a bit of thought. After five weeks of age, there is no stopping them. They will climb on you, maul your equipment, lick your camera lens, steal your light meter and generally create no end of trouble. The secret in dealing with this situation is that there is no secret, only patience.

(Ektachrome 100)

(Kodachrome 25)

Exposing for detail when the subject is black often causes   (Plus-X)
a loss of detail in areas that are white.

Making a Picture

If you have been asked to take pictures of a litter of eight-week-old puppies, your preparation should include dressing in the kind of attire which will allow you to lie on the ground (at puppy level). Be sure to take lots of film. My expectation for puppy pictures is one good picture for every twenty taken. Remember to bring the zoom lens. As puppies dart from place-to-place, you can remain stationary and keep the image area filled with the subject. Props are also important. Use a rumpled blanket; objects to climb in and out of; an old shoe and (if mother dog isn't around), bring out the friendly, family cat—puppies can't resist inspecting a cat.

Be cautioned that the puppies will pull on your hair, untie your shoelaces and take great pleasure in sinking their needle sharp teeth through your clothes; but it's all worth it. The only thing more enjoyable than a good photograph of a puppy is the puppy itself.

The black dog (Kodachrome 100)

CHAPTER FOUR

SPECIAL PROBLEMS

Predictability is always the principal concern with animal photography. The ability to control your subject for that split second when light meets film is paramount to achieving satisfying results. Fortunately, as we have seen, there are effective strategies for playing into a dog's intelligence and keen array of senses. Effective planning ahead of time will help insure that what you see *is* what you get. Beyond this, there are a few other "special problems" unique to dog photography. The most common of these are problems in correctly lighting a dark or black dog, stopping a dog in motion, photographing a big and a little dog together, photographing more than one dog at the same time, and working with an uncooperative dog.

The Black Dog

Dog coats that are brindle, blue or black present special exposure difficulties, especially when posed with people or objects that are a lighter color. Black literally "sucks up" the light. In some ways correcting exposure for the black dog is a no-win situation. If you take an average exposure reading, most of the detail in the dog will be lost. If you expose correctly for the black dog, the rest of your image will probably appear overexposed or washed out. You can, for example, appreciate the complexity of taking a properly exposed photograph of black and yellow Labrador Retrievers together.

Although difficult, it is possible. Even a simple "point and shoot" 35mm camera can be used to produce satisfactory results if the camera operator remembers to position the dark coated dog on the sun side of the lighter coated dog. Better yet, find a place where the lighter dog can be seated in shade, such as the perimeter shadow of a tree or building; then seat the dark coated dog in full sun. These suggestions should be secondary alternatives to using detached strobe light. If strobe is available, position the flash head so that it illuminates the dark coated dog only. Beware of positioning the flash so that it casts a shadow across the light coated dog.

Some corrective measures can be taken in the darkroom for both black & white and color negative film. The darkroom technician can "dodge" (hold back light) from the dark dog and burn-in (expose extra light) on the light dog. Since this is a remedial last resort, it is always better to solve the problem with the camera.

When shooting a black dog alone, the process of exposure is simplified. If you are using your camera in the manual mode, meter for surrounding (average) light conditions and then *open up the lens one additional full stop.* Opening the aperture a full stop will overexpose the area surrounding the dog, but you will be shooting tight anyway, so this shouldn't matter. The results of intentionally overexposing will bring out all the subtle detail in black areas that would be missed entirely with an exposure which averages the light over the entire image area. If you must rely on your camera's meter for correct exposure, be certain that the through-the-lens meter is centered on the black subject. Another way around the exposure problem is to trick the camera; that is, make the camera think that you are using a slower speed film than what is really in the camera. For example, if you photograph a black dog with ISO 200 film and the built-in light meter tells you that the average, correct exposure is f/11, and your goal is to have the camera automatically set the aperture for f/8 (because you want more light to reflect off the black dog) then you must manually manipulate the film speed indicator to ISO 100. Now the camera thinks (in a manner of speaking) that you are using slower film, and will automatically adjust by opening up the lens a full stop. Since you have really used ISO 200 film, the final image will be overexposed to your satisfaction.

Another thing to consider with dark subjects is contrast. If you are shooting a black dog and white dog together, do not use slow-speed, high-contrast film, since this film would accentuate the lightness and darkness of each subject. Film speeds of 200 ISO or greater are recommended to help reduce contrast.

Action Photography

Dogs and action photography fit well together, since unrestrained dogs outside their living area are almost always in motion. This does not mean, however, that you need to rely on luck. Your goal in selecting an outdoor sight is to locate an area which channels the dog's movement. A field surrounded by trees, nature walks where the path is a natural corridor, or a beach with water on one side and cliffs of the other all serve to confine or restrict the areas the dog may choose to move. Short of this, you will need to "think as the dog thinks." What objects or areas of an unrestricted, open space will the dog most likely choose to visit? Anticipate its decision, and be there with your camera ahead of time. For the first few minutes that most dogs are unleashed, they will dart from place to place in a frenzy of exploration by scent. Be patient. After five minutes or so, the dog will settle down and begin a new period of exploration by sight and sound. This is when its nose comes off the ground, making it a suitable subject for action photography.

You will want to make the proper adjustments for action photography by readying your equipment. A camera with a "fast" shutter speed is a must. Also, purchase film that lends itself to high speed photography (at least 400 ISO). Tripods are almost useless with moving objects, but a motor drive saves many pictures that would otherwise be lost while fumbling to recock the shutter. The indispensable motor drive allows you to shoot an entire roll of 24 exposures in less than 10 seconds (or faster with some cameras). Once again, the zoom lens is a valuable tool, since it allows you to compensate for the lack of control over a dog's decision to move at will.

(Ektachrome 100)

ISO 1000 negative film was used for this photograph. Fast film not only helps "freeze the action," but on a sunlit day, permits the photographer to shoot at small apertures — in this case f/16. Stopping down the lens widens the depth of field, and makes it far easier to keep a moving subject in focus.

Here is a rule to remember: the more parallel a moving object is to the film plane, the greater the chance of distortion. Stated another way: if a dog is running toward or away from you, it is less likely to appear blurred on the film than if it passes from one side to the other directly in front of the camera. Photographing some of the racing breeds, or dogs jumping in the air, may require the use of very fast shutters. I have been disappointed over film shot in a camera that was placed parallel to racing dogs and shot at a speed of 1/1000th of a second. Shutter speeds greater than this, however, should be sufficient to stop even the fastest dog at any position. If you are shooting Ektar color film, buy 1000 ISO. Meter and, if possible, shoot at 1/2000th of a second. Color quality will diminish with this film, but you will freeze the action.

Anticipation is another skill you will acquire. Attempt to visually predict the spot at which a jumping dog will reach its highest point; that split second, where the dog is actually neither climbing or descending. You won't often release the shutter at this exact "split second," but if you are even close you will catch the dog at a point where acceleration and deceleration have been greatly reduced. Since your trigger finger, eyes and brain must work in harmony, try to anticipate the peak of action *just before* it happens.

Panning is another technique that compensates for an object's movement as it appears in relation to the background. Panning allows you to ignore the background. This technique is frequently used at high-speed sporting events like bicycle or automobile races. The correctly panned image blurs the background, effectively separating it from the main subject. A good way to practice panning is by taking pictures of dogs running or jumping hurdles at obedience trials. Stand with feet firmly planted. Hold the camera steady and pre-focus on a point you estimate the subject will be when directly in front of you. Twist your torso from left to right (or vice versa) while following the subject and then release

Attempt to visually predict the spot at which a jumping dog will reach its highest point. (Kodachrome 25)

the shutter when it reaches the point of focus. Setting the correct shutter speed for panning is often a process of estimation. Ideally, the speed of the shutter should be fast enough to freeze the subject, yet slow enough to blur the background. Very fast shutter speeds will defeat your purpose, since the shutter will open and close so quickly that your body motion will not allow you to effectively blur the background. For the same reason, aperture settings are almost incidental since camera motion will negate depth-of-field.

Big Dog and Little Dog

Big and little subjects in the same picture is a challenge in composition. You will want to maximize the size of the small dog without cutting off the head or feet of the larger dog. There are several ways to approach the problem.

Big dog and little dog (Plus-X)

First, always place the smaller dog in the foreground.

Second, pose the dogs so that the larger dog is lying down and the smaller dog sitting or standing in front. If the larger dog must sit or stand, have the small dog sit on something, such as a rock or barrel, so that it is centered near the large dog.

Lenses can be used to solve the "Big Dog/Little Dog Problem." The picture on the opposite page was taken with a 105mm lens (a portrait lens) which tends to compress the subjects, giving the appearance of a bigger image. Wide angle lenses cause objects in the foreground to appear larger and objects in the background smaller.

More Than One Dog

This "Special Problem" should probably have been saved for last, because nothing else you will do in dog photography will be more challenging. If all the dogs you are shooting are obedience-trained, luck is certainly on your side. But even here there are no guarantees. Every additional dog increases the likelihood that one will have its eyes shut, tongue out or the like. Shoot lots of film; it is the only way to guard against this problem.

Chances are, you will not be shooting obedience-trained dogs. In this event you will need several people to help you. There should be at least one person for every dog, and an assistant to help with your instructions. Allow ample time before the shoot for the dogs to arrive and meet each other. This meeting and the photo session should be done on neutral territory. If you have more than one adult male dog in the photograph, they should not be seated near one another; place a female between them. This is not the time to allow any non-sense or bad attitudes. Never hesitate to impose order so that an aggressive or unruly dog understands that you are serious. Once two dogs get into a spat, you will be unable to take a photograph that does not show the tension in their eyes.

When the dogs have been satisfactorily arranged, be certain that the handlers remain with them until a second or two before you are ready to shoot. After the handlers have stepped aside, the dogs will quickly become aware of their freedom. You can gain a little time by placing their limbs in a way that makes it unnatural for them to arise without readjustment. If a dog is lying down, fold one paw underneath the pastern. If it is seated, pull a back leg underneath the body, so that it must be realigned before it can bounce to its feet. If you are shooting one of the double-jointed breeds, pull the back legs back toward the tail. With some clever attention-getting devices, you may gain a few more seconds while the dogs pay attention to your antics.

Obedience trained dogs are a pleasure.　　　　　　　　　　(Ektachrome 100)

Under the best of circumstances you will get no more than 10 to 15 seconds before at least one dog decides enough is enough. Bring the dogs back together and try again. After a few tries you will find that the dogs begin to understand. About 15 or 20 minutes attention is all you can expect from any group of untrained dogs.

The Impossible Dog

Barbara Woodhouse was right, there really are no bad dogs. But there are some *very* uncooperative dogs. If you have the patience and the time there is always a solution to taking pictures of any dog, no matter how uncooperative. As I have already mentioned, some dogs respond well to a firm grasp of the head, clear eye contact and a no-nonsense demand for their attention. The risk here is that an overly sensitive dog may respond by moping until you ask for forgiveness, or that the owner is sensitive and becomes unhappy. Then there are dogs that are just plain stubborn or have become the victims of indulgence by their owners. These are the dogs that can never be allowed off lead because they may never be seen again. You may also encounter a situation in which a valuable show dog's handler does not want to risk taking the dog off lead. In this case, leave the lead on and photograph the image as it is, or use a thin piece of monofilament fishing line as a leash. This thin line is strong enough to hold most dogs for a few seconds, yet virtually invisible to the eye. When all else fails, you might want to consider including a person in the photograph, so that the dog can be kept under control. Even a small child can control the average dog.

I should mention one other potential problem, the dog's owner. Dog owners can be every bit as difficult as parents at a Little League game. Those owners who are calm and understand the process of photography and your objectives, can be very helpful. Those owners who have their egos invested in the performance of their dog can be a nightmare. When you encounter this type of dog owner, you owe it to yourself and the dog to set firm ground rules, the most important of which may be that the owner leave the premises if you deem it necessary.

(Ektachrome 100)

Special Problems

Never set yourself up for disappointment by expecting that everything will go as planned; it never does. Even the most highly trained obedience dogs sometimes fail to cooperate. There is always another day.

And remember, given enough patience and planning, any photograph imaginable, is possible.

INDEX